Matthew Henson

JUNIOR ■ WORLD ■ BIOGRAPHIES

Matthew Henson

SEAN DOLAN

CHELSEA JUNIORS

a division of CHELSEA HOUSE PUBLISHERS

Chelsea House Publishers
EDITOR-IN-CHIEF: Remmel Nunn
MANAGING EDITOR: Karyn Gullen Browne
COPY CHIEF: Juliann Barbato
PICTURE EDITOR: Adrian G. Allen
ART DIRECTOR: Maria Epes
DEPUTY COPY CHIEF: Mark Rifkin
ASSISTANT ART DIRECTOR: Noreen Romano
MANUFACTURING MANAGER: Gerald Levine
SYSTEMS MANAGER: Lindsey Ottman
PRODUCTION MANAGER: Joseph Romano
PRODUCTION COORDINATOR: Marie Claire Cebrián

JUNIOR WORLD BIOGRAPHIES

EDITOR: Remmel Nunn

Staff for MATTHEW HENSON
PICTURE RESEARCHERS: Faith Schornick, Jonathan Shapiro
SENIOR DESIGNER: Marjorie Zaum
COVER ILLUSTRATION: Bradford Brown

First Printing

1 3 5 7 9 8 6 4 2

Library of Congress Cataloging-in-Publication Data
Dolan, Sean.
    Matthew Henson/Sean Dolan.
        p. cm.—(Junior world biographies)
    Summary: A biography of the black explorer who, together with Robert E.
Peary, discovered the North Pole in 1909.
    ISBN 0-7910-1568-8
    1. Henson, Matthew Alexander, 1866–1955—Juvenile literature.
2. Explorers—United States—Biography—Juvenile literature.
3. North Pole—Juvenile literature. [1. Henson, Matthew Alexander,
1866–1955. 2. Explorers. 3. Afro-Americans—Biography.
4. North Pole.] I. Title. II. Series.
G635.H4D65 1992
919.8—dc20   90-20458
[B]   CIP
[92]   AC

Contents

*An Eskimo family in Greenland converses and plays
outside its tent, which is made from the skins of seals.
During the summer, Eskimos often lived in tents
instead of in igloos.*

1

"Ahdoolo!"

Ahdoolo! . . . Ahdoolo!" The nonsense words echoed across the frozen wilderness of the northwest coast of Greenland. It was the very early morning of an April day, 1895. Inside their igloo, the Eskimos began to stir. Outside, as the dogs began to howl and scrap with one another, the man called out again: "Ahdoolo! Ahdoolo!" The Eskimos slowly rose, rubbing the sleep from their eyes. "Ahdoolo! Ahdoolo!" the man cheerfully yelled again. The Eskimos began to laugh and called back to him, "Ahdoolo! Ahdoolo!"

These words meant nothing to the Eskimos in their own language. They had begun to realize that the words also had no meaning in their friend's native language, for when he spoke them to his light-skinned companions they failed to respond. But the Eskimos understood what their always cheery friend meant when he called out "Ahdoolo! Ahdoolo!" each morning. He was saying, "Get up, get up. It is late, the sun is already up, and we have much work to do and many miles to go before we can sleep again."

The Eskimos loved this man, whose name was Matthew Henson. He was 29 years old, a black American from Washington, D.C. This was the second time he had visited them, and they knew very well that he was humble, brave, smart, and tremendously strong. In this frozen region of the world, where survival was so difficult, all of these qualities were highly prized. The Eskimos who lived here had grown used to being visited by outsiders. Some of the visitors were scientists, men who came to study the strange environment.

These men sometimes asked a lot of questions, but mostly they spent their time looking into a bunch of strange gadgets. The Eskimos found these men difficult to understand. The outsiders would tell them that they were recording the temperature of the air, for example. The Eskimos did not understand why this was necessary or useful. The position of the sun and the howling of the wind as it rushed over the ice told the Eskimos all that they needed to know. Soon it would be winter, the time of the long nights, and it would be much more difficult for them to hunt and to feed their families.

Most of the visitors were even harder to understand. They wanted to leave as soon as they arrived, but they did not wish to return home. No, they wanted to go even farther north on the ice, to regions where even the Eskimos feared to travel. They wanted to leave the safety of land and cross the frozen sea, all in search of something they called the North Pole. The Eskimos could not imagine why anyone would wish to do this.

There were no animals there to hunt, no friends, no family. There were no villages, where inside one of the snug, compact snow houses known as igloos a grandfather, his son, the son's wife, and several children could warm themselves around a fire and tell each other stories. Besides, the Eskimos believed, the ice near the North Pole was watched over by an angry, jealous devil named Kokoyah. Kokoyah did not like anyone trespassing on his territory. Those men who were foolish enough to disobey Kokoyah were usually severely punished.

Matthew Henson was one of these men who foolishly wished to reach the North Pole, but the Eskimos loved him anyway. He was not like the other *kabloona*, which was the word the Eskimos used for outsiders. *Kabloona* means "white person," but on Henson's first trip to the north, in 1891, the Eskimos were delighted to discover that he was dark skinned, like them. Some even thought that he must be a long-lost relative. In fact, an Eskimo man named Ikwah and his family "adopted" Henson. They insisted that he come and live with them in their igloo for a little while. It was from this family that Henson learned to speak the Eskimo language, and they also taught him much about how to survive in the freezing Arctic.

The Eskimos loved Henson for other reasons as well. The white men who came to the Arctic often acted as if they were superior to the Eskimos, even though they needed the help of the Eskimos if they were to succeed with their missions. The Eskimos had built a remarkable culture that enabled them to survive in one of the harshest environments on earth. The kabloona wanted the Eskimos to guide them and to help carry their supplies, but they did not consider the Eskimos their equals. Robert Peary, Henson's boss, believed that in some ways the Eskimos were little better than animals.

Henson looked at the Eskimos differently, perhaps because he, too, had been discriminated against. (In this case, to be discriminated against means to be judged negatively simply because of the color of one's skin.) In the society where he had grown up, discrimination and prejudice were commonplace. Fewer than 40 years earlier, black men had been bought and sold as slaves in the southern states. Abraham Lincoln, the 16th president of the United States, had ended slavery by issuing the Emancipation Proclamation, but in many places in the United States black men and women were still treated as inferior to whites. They were forced to attend separate schools and travel in separate railway cars, for example. They were forced to drink from separate water fountains and to use separate bathrooms. Many restaurants would not serve food to blacks. At sporting events, blacks would be made to sit in their own section of seats. Many white employers would not hire blacks for a job, and many universities would not accept blacks to study on their campuses. In most cities of the country, blacks could not expect to buy a house or rent an apartment in neighborhoods where whites lived.

Matthew Henson wearing the clothing made of furs that he used to protect himself from the icy winds and freezing temperatures in the Arctic.

Matthew Henson had experienced this discrimination many times. Even in the Arctic, he had been treated unfairly because of the color of his skin. Although the commander of the expedition, Robert Peary, admitted that Henson was his most trustworthy and valuable comrade, the other men of the expedition were paid $80 or $100 a month, and Henson received only $40. Henson was responsible for building the sleds that the expedition members used for traveling and to carry supplies. He was the expedition's best man at handling the dogs used to pull the sleds, a skill he had learned from his Eskimo friends. He was the expedition's most tireless traveler, and several times he had rescued members who had gotten lost on the ice. He sometimes acted as medic. Yet in newspaper accounts of the expedition's achievements, Henson was rarely mentioned. When he was, he was dismissed simply as Peary's "colored servant."

Perhaps because he was used to being criticized or overlooked because his skin was not white, Henson was able to see the Eskimos as people. In some ways they were different from him, but not inferior. Many of the kabloona, including Peary, pretended to befriend the Eskimos in order to gain their trust and help, but Henson genuinely loved and appreciated them. The Eskimos returned his affection. They called him Miy Paluk, which meant "my little Matthew" in their language. When he visited their villages, it was an occasion for celebration. His sunny smile and cheerful good nature brightened their igloos, and he regarded them as friends. When the Eskimos sang and danced for him, as was their tradition for guests, he responded by playing his accordion for them and singing them hymns he had learned as a boy.

So when Henson called out "Ahdoolo! Ahdoolo!" that morning in early April 1895, the Eskimos responded quickly to his comical cry. Because he had gotten to know and trust them, they knew and trusted him. The Eskimos had agreed to accompany Henson and Peary and one other man, Hugh Lee, on their latest adventure. The three explorers planned to travel by dogsled from their camp at Baffin Bay, across the northernmost portion of Greenland. They hoped by doing so to find a route to the North Pole, which no one had ever reached. Although the Eskimos believed that this plan was foolish, like most of the kabloona's doings, they had agreed to help carry supplies because Henson had asked them to.

Outside the igloo, the wind howled. It was springtime in the Arctic, but it was still bitterly cold. At night, the temperature sometimes dropped to 50 degrees below zero, and in the daytime it got only a little warmer. Henson, Peary, Lee, and the Eskimos breakfasted on *pemmican*, an unappetizing mixture of sun-dried walrus meat, raisins, and other fruit. Quickly, the Eskimos and Henson hitched the 42 sled dogs to their traces, as the long leather lines that fastened the dog team to its sled were known. With a sharp crack that echoed across the frozen tundra, Henson flicked the tip of his long whip above the head of the lead dog on his trace, just as the Eskimos had taught him to do. Suddenly, the pack of snarling, yowling, fighting dogs was transformed into a team, all pulling together. The dogs continued to bark as the sleds moved across the ice, north toward the Pole.

Henson in suit and tie aboard a ship. The years he spent at sea gave him the rare opportunity to learn about different peoples and cultures from experience and helped make up for his lack of a formal education.

2

At Sea

Matthew Alexander Henson was born on August 8, 1866, on his parents' farm in Charles County, Maryland, not far from the Potomac River. The Civil War had ended a little more than a year before Henson was born. One result of the war was that slavery was forbidden in all the states of the United States. Henson's mother and father had never been slaves, but they were still hopeful that the years after the war would be a period of freedom and equality for all blacks. Just two months before Matthew was born, Congress had proposed in the Fourteenth Amendment that all people born in the United States, whether their skin was white or black, be treated as citizens. If enough of the states agreed to this legislation—a process called ratification—for the first time blacks would be allowed to exercise such rights as voting and holding political office.

It would be a long time before America was able to fulfill this promise to its nonwhite citizens. Many white Americans had no intention of allowing blacks their freedom, no matter what the Constitution said. Throughout the country, but particularly in the southern states, white racists joined together to prevent blacks from owning their own land, from voting, or from running for office. They did this by forming organizations designed to terrify blacks into submission. The most infamous of these groups was the Ku Klux Klan, which was formed in 1866, the same year that Henson was born. Its members draped themselves in white sheets and burned crosses at night on the property of blacks whom it wished to frighten. Often, the Klan and other groups like it kidnapped and lynched blacks. All these hateful actions were designed to send an equally hateful message: that whites were superior, and that blacks would be allowed to enjoy their new freedom only as second-class citizens.

A year after Matthew was born, the violence against blacks in Charles County grew so severe that the Hensons were forced to move to Georgetown, then a poor section of Washington, D.C., the nation's capital. Then, when Matthew was just seven years old, his mother died. His father believed that his young son would be better off in a home where both parents were still living, so he sent Matthew to live with an aunt and uncle who lived nearby.

For Matthew, the high point of these years came when he was 10 and his uncle took him to a ceremony honoring Abraham Lincoln. Many blacks were grateful to Lincoln for having freed the slaves. At the ceremony, Matthew listened to an eloquent speech given by Frederick Douglass. Douglass had once been a slave. He escaped from his owner in 1838 and went on to write his autobiography, a book that convinced many white Americans that slavery was an evil that had to be eliminated. For many years prior to the Civil War, he edited a newspaper in Rochester, New York. The *North Star*, as Douglass called his paper, became one of the leading abolitionist publications. (To be an abolitionist meant to be in favor of an end to slavery.) For many American blacks, Douglass was a symbol of pride and achievement.

On the day that young Matthew Henson heard him speak, Douglass was at his fiery best. All blacks must do their part, Douglass said, to overcome prejudice and injustice. The best way for them to do so, he continued, was to make something of themselves by getting as much education as they could. Matthew was most impressed by his words.

But Douglass's words were hard to follow. Matthew was bright and a good student, but when he was 13 years old his father died. His aunt and uncle were no longer able to care for him, so Matthew was on his own. Fortunately, he had never been afraid of hard work. He was

As a young boy, Henson went to hear Frederick Douglass (below) speak. Douglass had escaped from slavery in 1838, when he was 20 years old. He became one of America's most forceful supporters of abolition, as the movement to end slavery was known.

able to get a job as a waiter at a restaurant where he had sometimes washed dishes as a summer job. The restaurant's owner was a kind woman whom most people called Aunt Jenny, but it was still a hard life for a boy. Matthew worked long hours, sometimes until very late at night. When he was done, Aunt Jenny let him sleep in the kitchen, where the cooks fed him leftover food.

A couple of years of this life was enough for Matthew. He was sure that life had better things in store for him, and he decided that he wanted to see the world. One of the regular diners at the restaurant was a sailor known as Baltimore Jack. This old salt often entertained his fellow patrons with tales of his adventures on the high seas. Matthew, who loved listening to these stories, thought that he would try the sailor's life. In the summer of 1879 he walked 40 miles to the city of Baltimore with little more than the clothes on his back. Matthew knew that ships from all over the world docked at the harbor in Baltimore.

On the waterfront, Matthew approached a gentleman who had been pointed out to him as the captain of the *Katie Hines*, a steamship. He asked this man, whose name was Captain Childs, if he could have a job as a cabin boy. The captain was impressed by Henson's confident manner and intelligent way of expressing himself and said yes. To his surprise, Matthew learned that his restaurant experience would serve him well at sea. His first assignment was peeling potatoes for the ship's galley.

His work quickly became more interesting. Over the next five years, the *Katie Hines* sailed around the world. It docked at ports in Africa, Russia, China, France, Japan, and many other places. These travels gave Henson the opportunity to see many different countries and observe how other people lived. Captain Childs also taught Henson a great deal. The captain quickly realized how eager Henson was to learn, so he gave him daily lessons from geography and history books. Henson also learned carpentry, first aid, and other skills. By the time the *Katie Hines* returned to Baltimore in 1885, he had become an extremely capable seaman.

In 1887, Henson journeyed to Nicaragua as a member of an expedition commanded by Robert Peary. The purpose of the expedition was to survey a route through the jungle for a canal that would link the Atlantic and Pacific oceans.

3

Planning
the Canal

Captain Childs had died near the end of the *Katie Hines*'s voyage. Henson found life at sea less enjoyable without the captain, who had always encouraged him, even when Henson grew discouraged because of racial slurs hurled at him by various members of the crew. Several times, Henson decided to end his studies because he believed that white people would always look down on him because of his color, no matter how great his achievements. But the captain was always able to convince him to continue his work to improve himself.

After the captain's death, Henson sailed on a couple of other ships, but he was no longer really happy at sea. Several members of the crews of these ships treated him badly because he was black, so Henson decided to try a different way of life. For the next three years he lived in several places in the eastern United States, where he worked at whatever job he could get. At different times he worked as a messenger, a night watchman, a dockworker, a chauffeur, and a bellhop. Finally, he returned to his old hometown of Washington, D.C., and took a job in a hat store, B. H. Steinmetz and Sons. Henson took pride in his work, but he never felt that any of these jobs was exactly right for him. He always believed that better things were on the horizon. But unlike some people, he was never content just to dream of a brighter future. When he was not happy with his situation, Henson was willing to take a risk to make it better.

In the spring of 1887, Henson had been working in the hat store as a clerk for 18 months. One day an unusual visitor came by the store. He said that his name was Robert Peary and that he was a lieutenant in the Civil Engineer Corps of the U.S. Navy. He was looking for a sun helmet, because in a short time he was going to lead an expedition through the jungles of Nicaragua. Nicaragua is a small country that occupies a central place on the narrow body of land (called an isthmus) that connects North and South America. Peary's job was to search the dense jungle for a possible route for a canal that would be dug across the length of Nicaragua. This canal would connect the Atlantic and Pacific oceans.

Both the U.S. government and the business community regarded Peary's mission as extremely important. In those days, before the airplane was invented, all foreign travel and commerce had to be done by ship. A ship that wanted to go from New York City to San Francisco, for example, first had to travel south all the way around the tip of South America before it could go from the Atlantic Ocean to the Pacific Ocean. The same was true, of course, for ships wishing to go from the Pacific to the Atlantic. This was tremendously inconvenient because it added a great deal of unneccessary time to such voyages. If a canal connecting the Atlantic and the Pacific could be dug, it would shorten the length of these voyages by more than half.

Peary was not normally a talkative man, but he told Mr. Steinmetz that he needed to hire a personal servant for the expedition. Steinmetz volunteered that he knew just the man, and he indicated the young clerk who was bringing Peary's sun helmet to the counter. Peary asked Henson if he would be interested, but he warned him that the pay would be low, the hours would be long, and the living conditions would be primitive. Henson had endured all sorts of adventures while at sea, so Peary's warnings did not worry him much. He knew that he was qualified to be much more than Peary's servant, but he recognized that this was a rare opportunity. He said yes.

In Nicaragua, Peary supervised a group of 45 engineers and surveyors and 100 black laborers from Jamaica. This work force was divided into six separate teams. The job of the laborers was to hack a course through 170 miles of the steaming Nicaraguan jungle. The engineers and surveyors were to take measurements of the treacherous terrain and to draw maps. Henson's major responsibility was to do Peary's laundry, but he quickly showed himself to be much more valuable. Peary saw that his servant was extremely intelligent, and he put Henson in charge of building a headquarters for the expedition. Henson did excellent work, and he made several improvements on the plan Peary had given him.

Soon, a better opportunity arose. The jungle was full of all sorts of hazards, such as snakes, swarms of mosquitoes whose bite could give a man the feared disease known as malaria, and hidden swamps. One day the chainman on one of the crews returned to camp in terrible condition. He had sunk in quicksand all the way up to his chest before he was rescued, and he was frightened half out of his wits. He refused to go back into the jungle. Henson saw a chance for himself, and he volunteered to take the man's place.

A chainman is responsible for holding the chain that a surveyor uses in taking measurements of a piece of land. The job requires a steady hand and enormous patience because the chain must remain perfectly straight at all times. If the chainman moves even to brush away a couple of bloodthirsty mosquitoes, for example, the measurement will be ruined. Henson excelled at the job despite the hazards and tiring heat of the jungle. He was soon made Peary's personal chainman, and he also learned several other skills. He became a crack shot with a rifle and an expert handler of canoes.

Henson spent six months in the jungle with the Peary expedition. Despite the hardship he and all the men had endured, he was disappointed when the expedition ended. He believed that he had been given the chance to do meaningful work, but he doubted that he would have the same opportunity in the United States, where good jobs were difficult for a black man to obtain.

One day on the return voyage, Peary asked Henson to come to his cabin, where he told him that he had done an excellent job. This was the first time that Peary had commented on Henson's work. The quiet lieutenant now made a startling announcement. His next mission would be to attempt to reach the North Pole, if he could obtain money and permission from the navy. How did Henson feel about coming with him? Once again, Peary warned Henson of the dangers involved in such a mission. Life in the jungle had been tough, but the Arctic could be much more dangerous. Temperatures sometimes got as cold as 60 degrees below zero, and the explorers would have to get used to a bleak landscape of ice and snow.

None of this bothered Henson. He had visited the Arctic on the *Katie Hines* and on another ship, and he felt sure of his ability to cope with any sort of physical discomfort. More important, he realized that no man had ever reached the North Pole. The first to do so would be as famous as Christopher Columbus. He had studied Peary and knew how determined the lieutenant could be. Now Peary told him that it had always been his dream to reach the Pole. Henson knew that he could never forgive himself if he let this chance slip away.

This massive glacier overlooks one of the many fjords, or narrow inlets of the ocean, along the coastline of the island of Greenland.

4

On the Ice

It took Peary three years to organize the North Pole expedition. During that time, Henson worked at a number of different jobs, including one as a messenger at the naval yard in Philadelphia, where Peary was stationed. He also read up on Arctic exploration, particularly on the adventures of Adolphus Greeley, who in fewer than 10 years earlier had set a record for reaching the northernmost point ever attained. But Greeley's achievement had been marred by tragedy, for 16 of the 23 men of his expedition had died on the ice caps just west of Greenland. Peary and Henson intended to learn from the costly lesson of the Greeley expedition.

Henson also discussed the expedition with Peary and learned that Peary had visited Greenland once before but that for various reasons this earlier expedition had been a failure. This time, Peary told Henson, he intended to do things differently.

To begin with, only a handful of men, just six in all, would make the journey. Part of the problem with expeditions like Greeley's was their large size, because in the Arctic, obtaining and transporting supplies for 23 men was very difficult. Peary's men would travel light. They would obtain most of what they needed from the Eskimos, whose way of life Peary wanted them to emulate in certain ways. The expedition would hunt for its food and kill the same animals that the Eskimos did in order to survive—walrus, seal, caribou, polar bear, and musk oxen. They would not carry tents to sleep in but would build igloos, as the Eskimos did. They would not carry sleeping bags, but would wear the same kind of animal furs as the Eskimos, which would also keep them warm when they slept. All traveling would be done by dogsled, just as the Eskimos did it.

Peary's ship, the *Kite*, landed on Greenland's west coast in June 1891. By that time, Henson had already discovered how many different tasks he would be expected to perform. On the voyage to Greenland, he did cooking and carpentry work. Then, a few days before the *Kite* landed, it was battered by huge sheets of ice in Baffin Bay. One broke the ship's rudder off, which in turn sent the tiller flying. Peary was struck by the tiller, and he wound up with a broken leg. Dr. Frederick Cook, a member of the expedition, set Peary's leg, and Henson used his carpentry skills to make a pair of crutches for the expedition's leader.

The broken leg did not affect Peary's determination to reach the Pole. As soon as the *Kite* landed, the other five men of the expedition began

Several dog teams and sleds travel across the Arctic ice. Notice how the dogs fan out to pull their loads rather than work side by side in pairs of two along a tight column. This makes pulling easier, but it is possible only in landscapes where there are no trees or other obstacles.

work on their various tasks. Henson was assigned to build a living quarters, and by himself he built a small house out of stone, sod, canvas, and tar paper. This house was divided into two rooms. One was for Henson, Dr. Cook, Langdon Gibson, John Verhoeff, and Eivand Astrup. The other was

for Peary and an unexpected seventh member of the expedition, his new bride, Josephine.

Once the house was complete, Henson set out to learn how to survive in the Arctic. It was then that he met the Eskimos, especially the family of a man named Ikwah, who became his good friend. The Eskimos taught Henson how to hunt for food and kill the large and often fierce animals that roam the frozen northern regions. They also taught him how to drive a dogsled. He became the Peary expedition's best sledder, even though the Eskimos were very amused by some of his early efforts with the dogs. The Eskimos helped the Peary expedition by trading them dogs in exchange for items such as knives or tobacco.

Peary also had much work for Henson. He expected him to teach the rest of the expedition how to operate a dogsled and how to get a team of dogs to obey. He also needed Henson to build the expedition dogsleds, because the ones that the Eskimos used were too small. Henson's personality proved almost as valuable as his skills. In the Arctic, the period between September and February is a time of constant night. The sun virtually disappears. These winter months were a time of constant tension for the Peary expedition. They could do little work and were forced to spend almost all day together in extremely close quarters. Except for Henson and Peary, none of the men adjusted to the Arctic winter very well, but Henson's even-tempered, reliable personality helped them endure until springtime.

Finally, spring came. The weather grew warmer, and the daylight hours grew longer. The men could begin planning their dogsled trip across the ice. In teams of two, the men began hauling supplies to strategic locations along their planned route. These sites are known as caches. Henson usually worked with Peary. On one venture north, the two men were trapped in a snowstorm. The intense cold froze part of one of Henson's eyes, which caused him great pain and blurred vision for months to come.

At last, the supplies were all set out, and Peary was ready to begin his trip to the pole. To Henson's disappointment, he learned that only two men would go on this portion of the expedition and that the second would be Astrup, who was the best skier of the bunch. Yet Henson was always a team player, and he did not complain.

Peary's plan was to travel as far north as possible on Greenland's ice fields in order to discover whether they reached all the way to the North Pole. For three months, Henson waited anxiously with Josephine Peary and the rest of the men while the Eskimos insisted that Kokoyah, the ice devil, had swallowed the two crazy kabloona. During that time, Henson killed his first polar bear. He estimated that the immense white beast weighed more than 800 pounds. Another time, Henson and a group of his Eskimo friends almost had their boat overturned by a herd of angry walruses.

Finally, on August 5, Henson set out at the head of a search party to find Peary and Astrup. After a couple of days, they spotted the two men out on the ice cap. Most of their dogs had died, and the commander and the skier were tired and hungry, but they were happy even so. Although they had not reached the North Pole, they had managed to travel more than 1,200 miles across the ice, all the way to Greenland's northeast coast.

Peary was now convinced that the Pole could be reached, and he began making plans to return home so that he could organize a new, even better prepared expedition. The next time out, he told Henson, they were going to capture the greatest prize since Christopher Columbus's discovery of America.

Henson relaxes on top of one of the sleds he built for travel in the Arctic. In addition to his carpentry skills, Henson was an expert handler of a dog team.

The Peary expedition prepares to set out across the ice from Anniversary Lodge, its headquarters on the coast of Greenland.

5

The Strong
Survive

Upon his return to the United States, Peary received a lot of attention for his success in the Arctic. Newspaper reporters wrote that his feat was almost as good as reaching the North Pole, and he was treated like a hero. But few news stories mentioned all that Henson had done for the expedition. Mostly, he was mentioned only as Peary's "colored servant." Even Peary, in his diary, referred to Henson as "my faithful colored boy." But by the time the two men returned from their next trip, Peary was expressing a greater appreciation for Henson. He always said afterward that Henson was "the best man I had with me."

There was much work to do before they could return to Greenland, however. In order to raise money to mount a second expedition, Peary gave a series of lectures around the country. Henson helped out by driving a dogsled through town on the day of Peary's speech in order to drum up interest. For Peary's performance, the hall where he spoke was made to look like an Eskimo village. After he finished showing photographs of the Arctic expedition, Peary introduced Henson. Henson would then come onstage with his sled and dogs. Audiences loved it.

At a speech Peary gave in Philadelphia, Pennsylvania, Henson had an encounter that he enjoyed greatly. In the audience, he spotted a naval officer whom he had first met before going to the Arctic. The man had told Henson at that time that blacks could not withstand cold weather, and he had bet Henson $100 that Henson would lose several of his fingers and toes to frostbite. (Frostbite occurs when parts of the body are exposed to extreme cold for a long time. If the condition is not treated, the affected parts sometimes need to be amputated.) Henson joyfully showed the man that his hands and feet were intact, and the man wrote him a check for $100.

Peary's expedition sailed from Philadelphia on June 26, 1893, aboard a new ship, the *Falcon*. Along with Henson, Eivand Astrup and Josephine Peary again were willing to take on the Arctic. There were eleven new members as well. These included an artist to paint scenes of Arctic and Eskimo life, a taxidermist to stuff animal specimens for museums, and a doctor to take care of Josephine Peary, who was expecting a baby.

In Greenland, Henson again built the party a headquarters. This structure was larger than the one he built on the previous visit. Peary named it Anniversary Lodge, because it was constructed on the site where he and his wife had spent their wedding anniversary on their earlier journey. Shortly after it was completed, it became the birthplace of Marie Ahnighito Peary. Eskimos came from as far as 200 miles away to look at the white-skinned, blue-eyed little girl. They called tiny Marie the Snow Baby because of the lightness of her skin.

Henson also met up again with his Eskimo friends, including Ikwah. The Eskimos were very disappointed when Henson told them that he was too busy to go hunting with them. Peary needed him to build ten sleds in a hurry, he explained. The Eskimos had a solution. Who knew better than they did how to build a sled? With their help, Henson soon had his work completed, and he was soon able to join his friends on a hunt for walrus and polar bear.

Peary's plan was essentially the same as the last time. He and his men would spend the summer of 1893 setting up supply caches out on the ice. Then, after waiting out the endless Arctic winter, they would set out northward across the ice in the spring of 1894.

Trouble began almost immediately. The larger expedition required more supplies, and Peary was sorry that he had brought so many men with him. Astrup, Hugh Lee, and George Clark made up the first party that Peary sent out. About halfway up a huge glacier (a glacier is an enormous body of ice) the three men became trapped in a tremendous blizzard. With the wind howling and blowing snow around, they were unable to see where they were going. The wind finally became so powerful that it overturned their sleds, which were loaded with hundreds of pounds of supplies, and blew them and the men back down the side of the glacier. Clark sprained his back, and Astrup grew so weak from the cold that he was unable to move. Lee grew dazed and confused and simply wandered off.

Eskimos who had been traveling with the supply party arrived with the bad news at Anniversary Lodge. Peary and Henson immediately raced off to attempt a rescue. They knew that the three men would not be able to survive for long in the cold without shelter and supplies. At the

foot of the glacier, Peary and Henson strapped
the two injured men to sleds. Three days of hard
traveling brought them back to safety at Anniversary Lodge.

Henson wanted to start out right away in
search of Lee, who was still missing, but another
disaster kept him from doing so. A giant chunk
of ice broke off from an overhang and fell into

the sea, causing a tidal wave. This huge wave swept onto shore and swamped the camp near Anniversary Lodge. Two of the expedition's boats were destroyed, and many fuel containers were swept away. By the time Henson had finished leading the cleanup of the wreckage, another storm had hit. The raging winds and snow made travel out of the question.

Henson and two companions use a dogsled to transport supplies from the Falcon. *Had it not been for Henson's stamina and courage, several members of the Peary expedition would have died.*

The weather finally cleared, and Henson set out to look for Lee. Before he could leave, a party of Eskimos arrived at the camp. With them, strapped on a sled, was Lee. He was exhausted, starving, and badly frostbitten, but he was alive. He had wandered through the blizzard for almost a week without food before stumbling into a small Eskimo settlement.

It took Lee the entire winter to regain his strength. The long, dark months were even gloomier than might have been expected, for Peary was greatly worried about the success of the expedition. The accidents had prevented his men from placing supplies far enough ahead along their route, which meant that the springtime mission was not likely to succeed.

At last the weather grew warm enough for Peary and his men to set out. This time, Henson would be going with them. Again, blizzards slowed their progress. Astrup and Lee soon grew weak from cold and exhaustion, and Henson was forced to take them back to safety. Peary and a few others attempted to press on, but with little luck. The wind howled constantly, and the temperature dipped to 50 degrees below zero. Finally, Peary admitted defeat. When he ordered his men to turn around and head for Anniversary Lodge, they had made only 128 miles.

But Peary was far from beaten. The *Falcon* returned to Greenland in August, as Peary had arranged for it to do. The original plan was that the entire expedition would return to the United States aboard it, but Peary suddenly changed his mind. He announced that he would be staying in Greenland for another winter so that he could attempt to reach the North Pole again in the spring of 1895. He ordered his wife and baby to go home on the *Falcon*. The others, he said, were free to choose for themselves whether to go or stay.

Peary's ship trapped in the ice. Henson was one of only two men who volunteered to stay with Peary in the Arctic in the spring of 1895.

6

Tempting
Kokoyah

Only two men, Henson and Lee, volunteered to stay with Peary and test Kokoyah's patience once again. The men had all of the long winter to wonder whether they were making a foolish move. Because of the problems in setting out supplies, they would have to rely only on those provisions that they could carry with them on their sleds. All three knew that this could be very unwise, but they were determined to continue. When the weather permitted, Henson, Peary, and Lee hunted. They killed many walruses, from which they made a large supply of pemmican for the spring expedition.

The three men set off for the polar ice cap on April 1, 1895. Henson convinced some of the Eskimos to come with them to help carry supplies, but after a week the Eskimos told the kabloona that they were on their own. The whites were entering Kokoyah's territory, the Eskimos said. One of them, Ahnalka, begged Henson to turn back with them. Henson said that he had come this far and intended to see what lay ahead.

What lay ahead was danger and heartbreak. The wind blew fiercely, and temperatures reached a numbing 50 degrees below zero. In such chilling cold, even the simplest tasks become a great challenge. Under such conditions, the body is forced to burn most of its energy just to heat itself, leaving little left over for anything else. As a result, the three men quickly grew exhausted. It took tremendous concentration to keep from growing disoriented and depressed. The beautiful but monotonous Arctic landscape, with ice stretching out to the horizon in all directions, also contributed to their mental fatigue.

It was enough of a challenge just to move forward. Arctic ice is not smooth, like the frozen surface of a rink or skating pond. Instead, it is pitted and rutted, which made for a bumpy ride. Often, the surface was so rough that the sled became stuck, and the dogs could not pull it free. At those times, Peary, Henson, and Lee would have to get off the sled and push. Other times, the dogs would become tangled in their traces. Because there are no trees in Greenland, sled dogs do not have to run in a narrow, double-file column. They can be allowed to fan out in front of the sled, which makes pulling easier. This relative freedom, however, meant that the dogs often tangled their lines and the party would have to stop.

The group of three men moved slowly across the lonely Arctic landscape. Sometimes, when the wind was blowing ice and snow, they could only see a few feet in front of them. At other times it was too cold to travel at all, and they stayed huddled together in their igloo. As always, Henson was able to meet any challenges. He had the heaviest load to transport, but because he was so skilled at driving the dogs, he kept on overtaking Peary's sled. Finally, Henson suggested that he attach the leader's sled to his own, sort of like a trailer, and have both Peary's and his own dogs pull the load. This method enabled Peary to ski out ahead and set the trail, while Henson ably managed the 28 dogs pulling the 2 sleds.

Lee was extremely courageous, but he lacked the strength of the other two men and had trouble keeping up. One day, in a fearsome blizzard, he disappeared. It was more than two days before the winds died down enough so that Henson could go look for him. He found Lee huddled on his sled, nearly frozen to death and almost blind from the driven snow. His feet were so frostbitten that he could not stand, so he became a passenger on Henson's already overloaded sled.

But there was no question of turning back. Onward the men pressed. Food ran low, until there was no longer enough pemmican to feed to the dogs. Each night, Henson was forced to kill one of the dogs to feed to the others. After five weeks, the three men finally reached Navy Cliff, which was the farthest point Peary had reached on his previous journey. Only 11 dogs, 1 sled, and virtually no food had survived the expedition. Peary and Henson now both realized that they could not reach the North Pole. In fact, unless they could successfully hunt, they would not have enough food to make it back to Anniversary Lodge safely.

Fortunately, Henson had learned well the lessons the Eskimos had taught him. He was able to find a herd of musk oxen, and he and Peary shot several of the shaggy beasts. This gave them hundreds of pounds of meat for the return journey. All of it would be needed, for a sled dog at work can easily consume 7 to 10 pounds of meat every day.

The return trip was as difficult as the first leg of the journey had been. It took even longer, and the food did not last. The meat ran out when they were still 200 miles away from Anniversary Lodge, and the pemmican was gone soon afterward. Henson was forced to kill all but one of the dogs. While the men were still 120 miles away, Lee collapsed. He had been able to walk a little bit on snowshoes, but now he could go no farther. Henson and Peary were forced to put themselves in the traces of the one remaining sled in order to pull Lee to safety.

Near the end of June, the three men staggered into Anniversary Lodge. They quickly consumed the little bit of food there and collapsed. Only Henson was strong enough to continue. Recognizing that they would all die without food and medical attention, he bravely made his way to the nearby Eskimo village. His friends took one look at him and put him under the care of the *angeeco*, or medicine man. While Henson was recovering, the Eskimos took food and medicine to Peary and Lee. All three men were suffering from frostbite, exhaustion, hunger, and scurvy, which is a disease that results from a lack of vitamin C in the diet.

Under the angeeco's care, Henson soon felt much better. Peary rallied quickly, too, although his bitter disappointment at once again failing to reach the Pole kept his spirits low. Only Lee failed to bounce back. On August 3, 1895, the *Kite* arrived to carry the three men home. On board the ship, Lee received the medical attention he so badly needed. Peary's spirits picked up, too, even though he learned that a Norwegian explorer, Fridtjof Nansen, had recently sailed to within 226 miles of the North Pole. This was much closer than Peary had ever come, but Nansen's success only made Peary's determination to be the first one there grow stronger. And Peary now knew that he had an extremely valuable comrade he could always count on, for Matthew Henson had proved himself the equal of any of the men who had challenged the Arctic.

Triumph at the Pole: Atop an icy hill near the North Pole, Henson and his Eskimo friends hoist the American flag and several other banners.

7

All the
Way There

Henson and Peary returned to the Arctic four times between 1896 and 1908, but they could not reach the North Pole. The first two trips, made in 1896 and 1897, were the most successful. Using the *Hope* and a gigantic crane, Peary and Henson managed to remove a huge meteorite, weighing 35 tons, that had fallen on Greenland long ago. (A meteorite is a large particle of matter, similar to rock or stone, from outer space.) The meteorite immediately went on display in the Museum of

Natural History in New York City. It added to Peary's fame, but it did not make him feel any better about his failure to reach the North Pole.

The most frustrating trip began in 1898. Peary now had a new plan. Using a specially designed ship called the *Windward*, Peary planned to sail much farther northward along Greenland's coast before landing. This way, his party would not have to travel so far over land to reach the Pole. The *Windward* was supposed to have engines so powerful that it could batter its way through the Arctic ice.

The plan did not work. In the fall of 1898, the ship became hopelessly stuck in ice off Ellesmere Island, which is just to the west of Greenland. Peary announced a new scheme. The men would abandon the *Windward* and march to Fort Conger. The fort was on the northern shore of Ellesmere Island. It was also the place where the men of the Greeley expedition had waited in vain to be rescued.

In temperatures of 60 degrees below zero, Henson cut a trail through the ice to Fort Greeley. Although it was already winter, Peary insisted on starting out immediately. It was a bad mistake. This was a different sort of journey than any he and Henson had taken before. Beneath the ice this time was not land, as on Greenland, but the waters of the Arctic Ocean. At different spots huge and strangely shaped pressure ridges sprang up. These were created by the force of two bodies of ice crashing into each other, driven by the ocean currents beneath them. At night, Peary, Henson, and the four Eskimos who traveled with them could hear the ice groaning and creaking. Sometimes the explorers came upon huge open areas of water where the ice had opened up. They would then have to change direction to get around them.

Peary and Henson made it to Fort Conger, but at great cost. Peary's feet became badly frostbitten, and he was unable to walk. Henson strapped him to his sled and in only 11 days brought him the 250 miles back to the *Windward*, where the ship's doctor was forced to cut off all but the big toe on each of Peary's feet.

Despite this setback, Peary was determined to stay in the Arctic. He and Henson remained for four more years. During that time, they made three separate attempts at the Pole. All fell short. On April 21, 1902, Peary wrote in his journal, "The game is off. My dream of 16 years is ended. . . . I cannot accomplish the impossible." The discouraged explorers returned home.

Henson also thought that the quest had come to an end. Even before the last expedition, he had begun to tell friends that he was through with Arctic exploration, but his friend George Gardner had convinced him to continue by telling him how important it was for black Americans to have Henson as a role model. Blacks are proud of you and all that you have achieved, Gardner told his friend. Think how proud they will be if a black man reaches the North Pole. Still, Henson was glad to have a break from his polar labors. After he returned to the United States, he took a job on the Pennsylvania Railroad, which enabled him to see much of the country. He also asked his sweetheart, Lucy Ross, to marry him.

But Peary could not abandon his dream forever, and neither could Henson. In 1905, Peary set off on a new expedition, and Henson was with him. This time, a new ship, the *Roosevelt*, succeeded in smashing its way through the Arctic ice. Sledding over extremely treacherous ice, Henson and Peary came within 175 miles of the Pole. This was the closest that anyone had ever come. They returned to the United States both frustrated and certain that next time they would make it.

Peary and Henson's sixth polar expedition departed from Long Island, New York, on July 6, 1908. With the two men this time were four other adventurers. All of them were younger than the 42-year-old Henson, but Henson knew that his vast experience would more than make up for the youthful high spirits of his comrades.

This time the expedition had good luck right from the beginning. The weather was just cold enough to keep the surface frozen with a minimum of breaks in the ice, but not too cold to work and travel in. Henson wrote in his diary that he had never seen such smooth sea ice, and the group made rapid progress. After every five days, Peary sent one of the members of his party back to the ship. The final assault on the Pole would be made by just Peary, one other member of his expedition, and a couple of Eskimos. In this way, only a small load of supplies would have to be carried the entire length of the journey. But who Peary would ask to join him at the Pole remained a mystery.

The explorers continued on, averaging a very fast 16 miles a day. On March 28, 1909, they passed the farthest point north they had ever reached. Two days later, Peary asked the third remaining member of the expedition to return to the ship. Matthew Henson would go with him to the North Pole.

The next day, April 1, Peary, Henson, and four Eskimos, Seegloo, Ootah, Eginwah, and Ooqueah, began their final dash for the Pole, which was now 130 miles away. Because of his crippled feet Peary was traveling slowly, but Henson drove his lead team at a furious pace. On the morning of April 6, Henson woke up Seegloo and Ootah. "Ahdoolo! . . . Ahdoolo!" he called, a little more urgently than usual. They were just 35 miles from the Pole.

At Peary's orders, Henson and the two Eskimos forged ahead. They were supposed to stop just short of the Pole to let Peary catch up. That afternoon, when Henson stopped for a rest, he realized that he had made a mistake. If his calculation was correct, he had not only reached the Pole, but gone beyond it! He backtracked a little bit and waited for Peary. The commander of the expedition took out his instruments, took his readings, and announced in a matter-of-fact voice that at last, after so many years of hardship, they had reached their destination. Henson explained to Ootah, "We have found what we hunt." The Eskimo shrugged his shoulders, still unable to fully understand these strange outsiders from another part of the world. "There is nothing here," Ootah said. "Only ice."

With an American flag in his hand, Henson climbed to the top of a nearby pressure ridge. Peary snapped his picture. Then Henson helped set up camp. After a long night's sleep, the expedition headed home. Henson's exploring days were over.

The rest of Matthew Henson's life was frustrating in many ways. Peary was treated as a national hero, but Henson was slighted. Racist reporters asked Peary why he had allowed a Negro to accompany him to the North Pole. Peary, who was unwilling to share the credit for his achievement, made things worse with his answer. He had been forced to take Henson with him all the way, he said, because Henson was too ignorant to make it back to the ship on his own. This was completely unfair, of course, for many times it had been only Henson's courage and intelligence that saved the expedition from disaster. While Peary received large fees for giving lectures and was granted a rich pension from the government, Henson was forced to park cars in a Brooklyn garage to earn his living.

But Matthew Henson was not the kind of man to let bitterness ruin his life. He later got a good job with the U.S. Customs Bureau, and he lived a long, rich, and full life until he died in 1955, at the age of 88. During his final years he took satisfaction in his own knowledge of all that he had achieved. If any doubted him, there was always the picture Peary had taken at the North Pole.

That photograph showed Matthew Henson, a black American, with the flag of his country in his hand at the top of the world. And anyone who doubted his achievements could always ask the Eskimos, who for years afterward told legends about a very great man named Miy Paluk. The Eskimos even added a new word to their lan-

Only late in his life did Henson receive the recognition he deserved for his part in discovering the North Pole. Here, at age 87, he holds the flag of the Explorers Club. That same year, 1954, he was asked to address the club on the occasion of the 45th anniversary of the discovery of the Pole.

guage: The word *ahdoolo* came to stand for a very special kind of courage. It was used not only to mean bravery and endurance, but to mean the ability to face even the hardest work and the greatest challenge with hope and good spirits. It is a fitting word with which to remember Matthew Henson.

Chronology

1885	Returns to the U.S. and takes a job in Washington, D.C.
1887	Joins Robert Peary on an expedition to Nicaragua
1891	Makes his first voyage to Greenland with Peary, aboard the *Kite*
1893–95	Makes second trip to Greenland, aboard the *Falcon*; builds Anniversary Lodge; accompanies Peary on journey to northern Greenland
1896–97	Henson and Peary return to the Arctic aboard the *Hope* and recover a 35-ton meteorite
1898	Henson begins a four-year expedition in the Arctic with Peary
1902	Returns to the U.S. and takes a job on the Pennsylvania Railroad; becomes engaged to Lucy Ross
1905–6	Accompanies Peary on an expedition that travels to within 175 miles of the North Pole
1907	Marries Lucy Ross
1908	Expedition leaves New York to reach the North Pole
1909	Henson, Peary, and four Eskimos become the first people to reach the North Pole

1912	Henson's *Negro Explorer at the North Pole* is published
1913	Henson begins work for the U.S. Customs Bureau
1937	Elected to the Explorers Club
1945	Awarded medal from the U.S. Navy
1954	Invited to the White House by President Eisenhower
1955	Matthew Henson dies

Glossary

abolitionist   in U.S. history, particularly in the decades before the Civil War, a member of the movement to end slavery

ahdoolo   a nonsense word invented by Matthew Henson that has come to be used by the Eskimos to mean bravery and endurance

angeeco   the Eskimo word for medicine man

Arctic   the region around the North Pole

blizzard   a severe snowstorm

cache   a strategic site at which supplies are placed along a route

canal   a waterway built for navigation

chainman   the person responsible for holding the chain that a surveyor uses in taking measurements of a piece of land

discriminate to judge someone negatively because of the color of his or her skin

Emancipation Proclamation an order given by President Lincoln on January 1, 1863, freeing the slaves in the Southern states

Eskimos the native people who inhabit Greenland, Alaska, northern Canada, and part of northeast Siberia

expedition a journey undertaken for a specific purpose

Fourteenth Amendment added to the U.S. Constitution in 1868, a proposal that all people born in the United States, whether black or white, should be treated as equal citizens

frostbite a condition that occurs when parts of the body are exposed to the extreme cold for a long time

glacier a huge body of ice

igloo an Eskimo house made out of blocks of snow or ice

isthmus a narrow body of land that connects two other land masses

kabloona an Eskimo word for a white person

Kokoyah in Eskimo mythology, an angry, jealous devil who watches over the North Pole

Ku Klux Klan an organization formed in 1866 for the purpose of terrorizing blacks

lynch   to illegally hang a person by group action

malaria   a disease, characterized by chills and fever, that is caused by parasites and transmitted by mosquitoes

meteorite   a large particle of matter, like a rock or stone, from outer space

North Pole   the northernmost point of the earth

pemmican   a mixture of sun-dried walrus meat, raisins, and other fruit

pressure ridge   a raised strip of ice and snow formed by the force of two bodies of ice crashing into each other

scurvy   a disease, characterized by bleeding gums and loose teeth, that is caused by a lack of vitamin C

surveyor   a person who measures areas of land in order to draw up maps or plans

taxidermist   a person who stuffs and mounts animal skins

tidal wave   an unusually high ocean wave

traces   the long leather lines that fasten a dog team to its sled

tundra   a treeless plain with black muddy soil and a permanently frozen subsoil

Sean Dolan has a degree in literature and American history from the State University of New York. He has written and edited several books on exploration and other historical topics for young readers.

Picture Credits